Lo siento, robé tu gato

Gracias por alimentarla mientras estoy fuera

Marcy Schaaf

Spanish

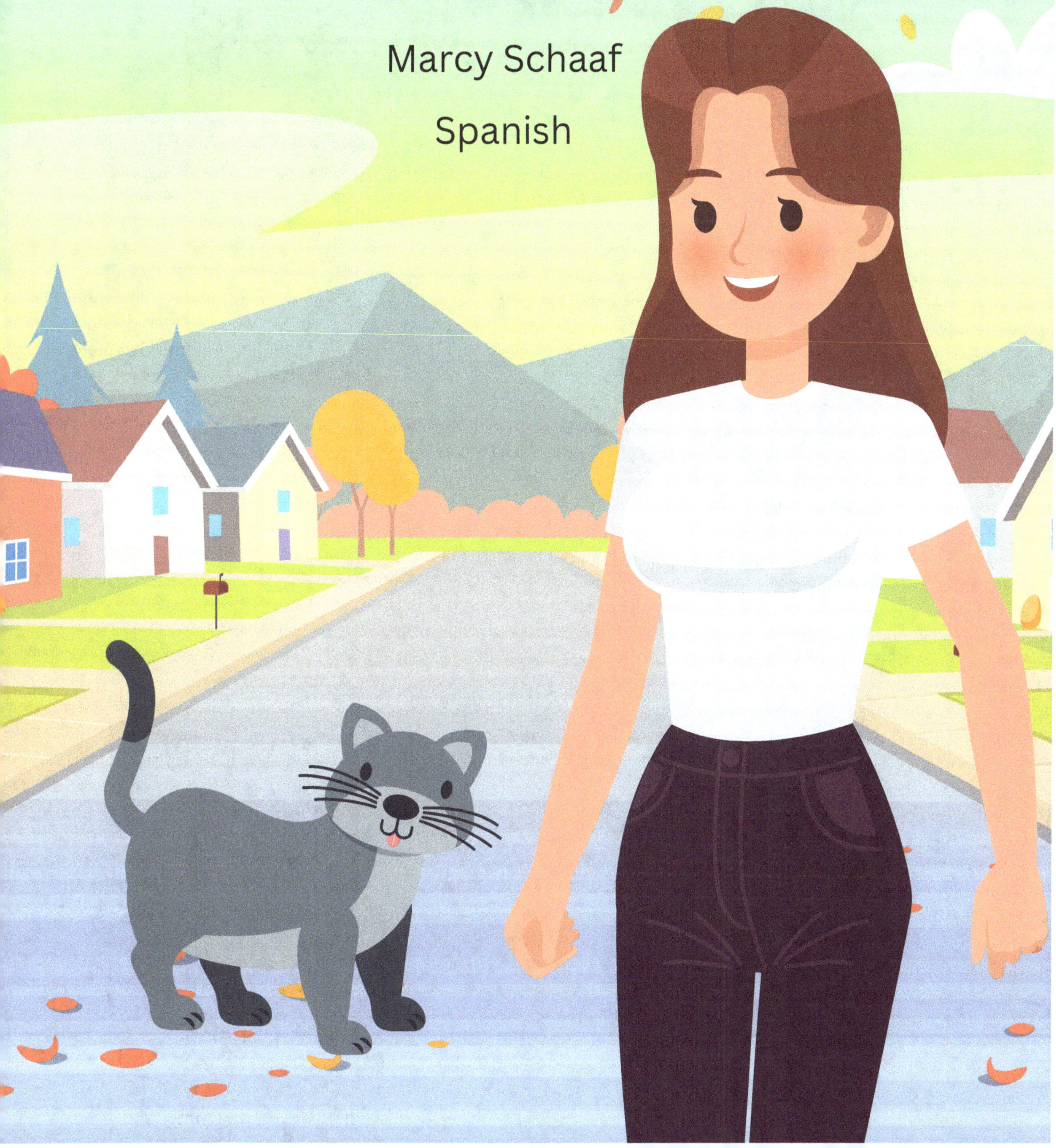

Sorry I Stole Your Cat

Thanks for Feeding Her While I'm Away

Marcy Schaaf

Meet Delila, the lovable cat whose life takes an unexpected turn when her family gets a new puppy. Feeling left out and overwhelmed, Delila finds a new home next door with a kind single lady. But when the lady goes on vacation, Delila's old family steps in to help, and everyone learns a valuable lesson about change and love.

Sorry I Stole Your Cat, Thanks for Feeding Her While I'm Away is a true story from Pahoa, Hawaii.

This delightful tale shows that even when life changes, it can still be filled with love, happiness, and new beginnings. Join Delila on her heartwarming adventure and discover that no matter what happens, it's okay to embrace change!

This book is dedicated to Lux and Tula, the amazing kids next door.

Thank you for sharing your wonderful cat, Delila, with such open hearts and allowing her love to fill my life. Your kindness and understanding meant the world to both of us. Delila brought joy and comfort to my home when I needed it the most, and I hope she brought just as much happiness to yours.

Life has a funny way of bringing us together in the most unexpected ways, and I'm so grateful that our paths crossed. Lux and Tula, your generosity and love made all the difference, and for that, I am forever thankful.

Your friend and Neighbor,
Marcy Schaaf

Copywrite2024 @Marcy Schaaf Sorry I stole Your Cat
Thanks for Feeding Her While I'm Alway

Once there was a cat named
Delila.

Había una vez una gata llamada Delila.

She lived with a family of four.

Vivía con una familia de cuatro.

Mom, Dad, a girl, and a boy.

Mamá, papá, una niña y un niño.

One day
they got a new puppy.

Un día consiguieron un nuevo cachorro.

The puppy ate Delila's food.

El cachorro se comió la comida
de Delila.

The puppy chased her around.

El cachorro la persiguió.

It even took her spot in bed!

¡Incluso ocupó su lugar en la cama!

Delila was old and
didn't wanna play with the puppy.

Delila era mayor y no quería jugar con el cachorro.

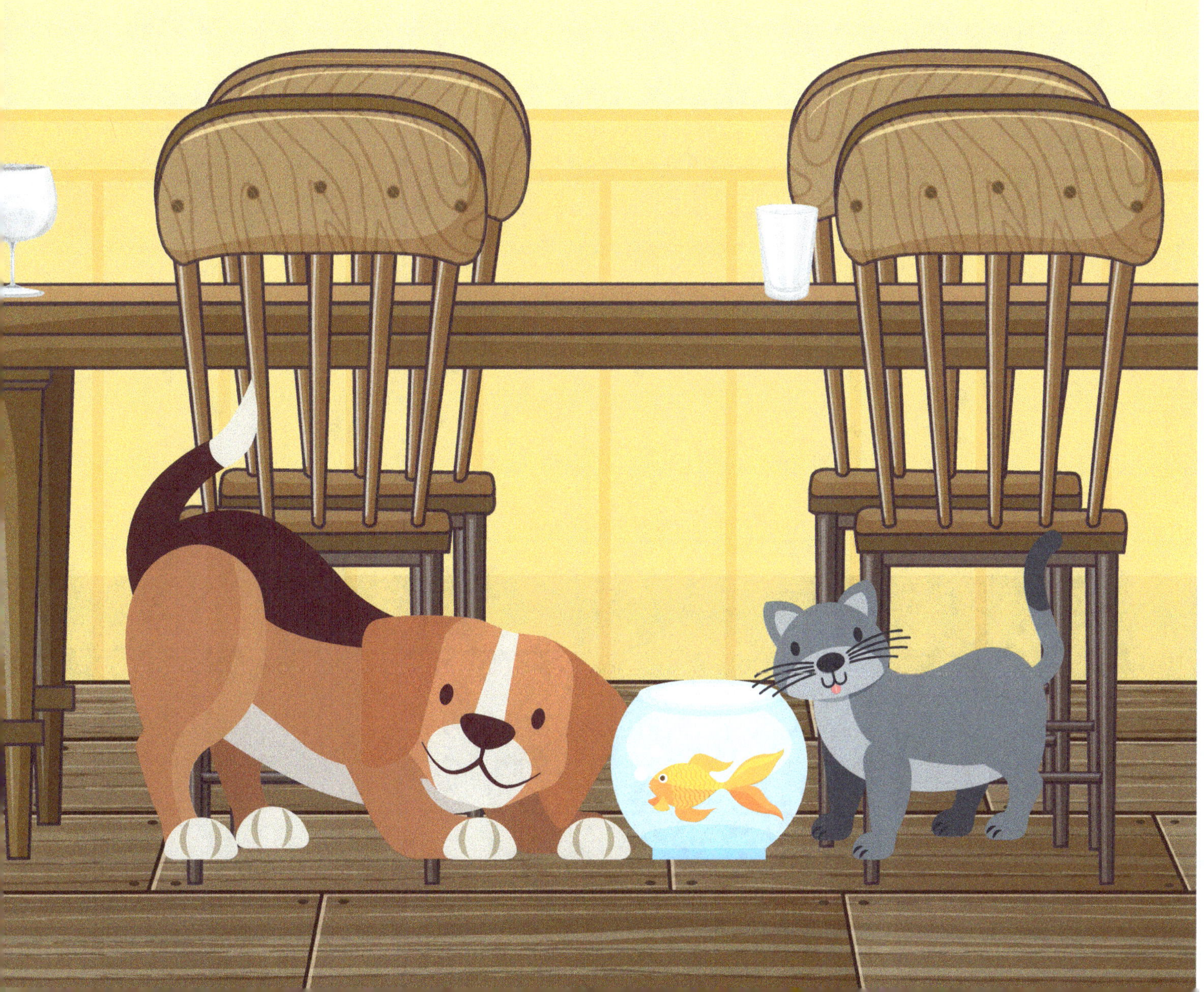

She found a peaceful
home next door.

Encontró un hogar tranquilo al lado.

A lady lived there alone.

Allí vivía una señora sola.

The lady planted catnip for Delila.

La señora le plantó hierba gatera
a Delila.

She gave Delila lots of love.

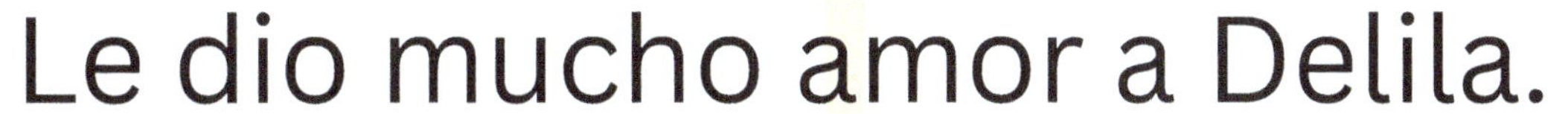

Le dio mucho amor a Delila.

Delila had a new comfy spot.

In the lady's master bedroom.

Delila tenía un nuevo lugar cómodo.

En el dormitorio principal de la dama.

One day the lady
went on vacation.
TRAVELER
TA

Un día la señora se fue de vacaciones.

She asked the kids
next door for help.

Pidió ayuda a los niños de al lado.

"Sorry I stole your cat," she said.

"Perdón, te robé el gato", dijo.

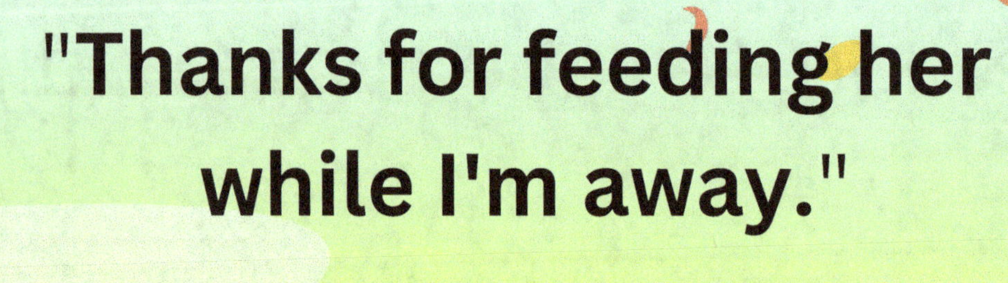
"Thanks for feeding her
while I'm away."

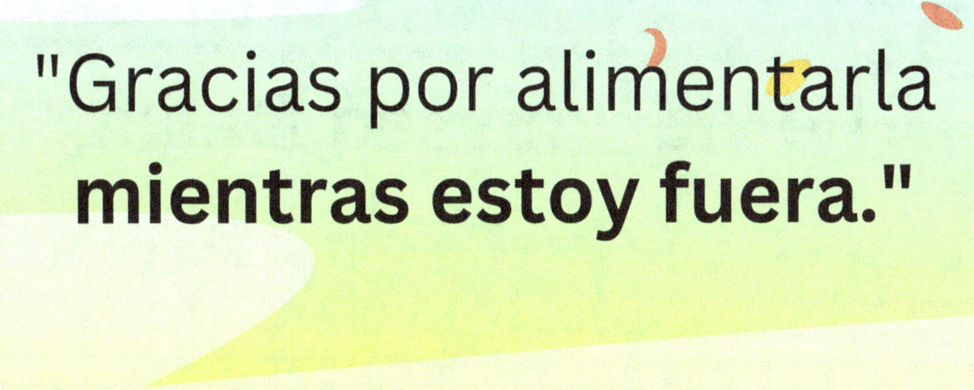

"Gracias por alimentarla
mientras estoy fuera."

The kids missed Delila.

Los niños extrañaban a Delila.

They were happy to help.

Estaban felices de ayudar.

They fed Delila every day.

Le daban de comer a Delila todos los días.

They played with her, too.

También jugaron con ella.

Delila felt loved and happy.

Delila se sintió amada y feliz.

She had the best of both worlds.

Tenía lo mejor de ambos mundos.

A quiet home and playful kids.

Un hogar tranquilo y niños juguetones.

When the lady returned,
she thanked them.

Cuando la señora regresó, les dio
las gracias.

Delila purred contentedly.

She was right where
she should be!

Delila ronroneó satisfecha.

¡Estaba justo donde debería estar!

Life changes sometimes
and that's okay.

La vida cambia a veces
y eso está bien.

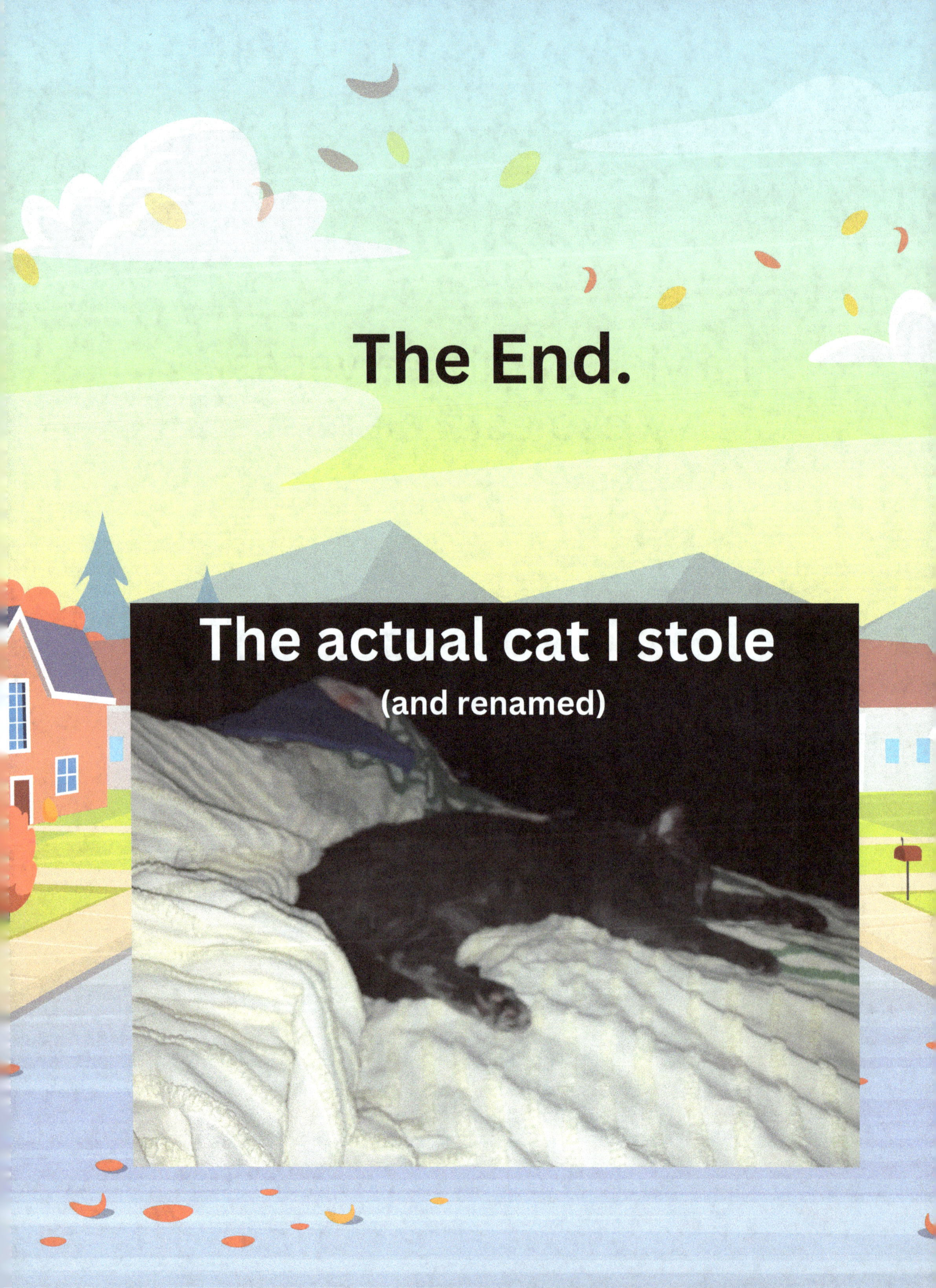

The End.
The actual cat I stole
(and renamed)

The real kids next door

Books By Schaaf

www.BookBySchaaf.com

Find us at: